A Tune a Day

A First Book

for

Flute Instruction

By

C. Paul Herfurth

and

Hugh M. Stuart

THE BOSTON MUSIC COMPANY

PUPIL'S DAILY PRACTICE RECORD

Pupil fills in number of minutes of daily practice.
Parent signs initials in space designated as certification of pupil's record for the week.
Teacher fills in grade for quality of each week's work as shown by the lesson. Teacher signs initials.

E – Excellent; G – Good; M – Medium, Distinctly Above Passing;
L – Low, Lack of Effort; F – Failing.

FIRST SEMESTER

Week	Mon.	Tues.	Wed.	Thur.	Fri.	Sat.	Parent's Initials	Weekly Grade	Teacher's Initials
1									
2									
3									
4									
5									

1st TEST GRADE

Week	Mon.	Tues.	Wed.	Thur.	Fri.	Sat.	Parent's Initials	Weekly Grade	Teacher's Initials
6									
7									
8									
9									
10									

2nd TEST GRADE

Week	Mon.	Tues.	Wed.	Thur.	Fri.	Sat.	Parent's Initials	Weekly Grade	Teacher's Initials
11									
12									
13									
14									
15									

3rd TEST GRADE

Week	Mon.	Tues.	Wed.	Thur.	Fri.	Sat.	Parent's Initials	Weekly Grade	Teacher's Initials
16									
17									
18									
19									
20									

4th TEST GRADE

SECOND SEMESTER

Week	Mon.	Tues.	Wed.	Thur.	Fri.	Sat.	Parent's Initials	Weekly Grade	Teacher's Initials
1									
2									
3									
4									
5									

5th TEST GRADE

Week	Mon.	Tues.	Wed.	Thur.	Fri.	Sat.	Parent's Initials	Weekly Grade	Teacher's Initials
6									
7									
8									
9									
10									

6th TEST GRADE

Week	Mon.	Tues.	Wed.	Thur.	Fri.	Sat.	Parent's Initials	Weekly Grade	Teacher's Initials
11									
12									
13									
14									
15									

7th TEST GRADE

Week	Mon.	Tues.	Wed.	Thur.	Fri.	Sat.	Parent's Initials	Weekly Grade	Teacher's Initials
16									
17									
18									
19									
20									

FINAL GRADE

_____
Name

_____
School

_____
Address

_____
Grade

FOREWORD TO TEACHERS

IN compiling this course the objective has intentionally been not to cover too much ground, but rather to concentrate on the acquisition of a thorough musical background on a solid foundation in good flute playing. These two requisites are inseparable.

A brief section is devoted to the simpler rudiments of music which should be thoroughly understood as the need arises.

The learning of the positions and fingerings as introduced should be insisted upon.

Cultivate in the pupil the habit of careful listening.

The familiar hymns and folk-songs have been selected because of the melodic interest as pieces, and because, in addition, each one offers some technical point to be mastered.

The value of learning to "think count" from the very beginning cannot be over-estimated. Only in this way can a pupil sense rhythm. Rhythm, one of the most essential elements of music, and usually conspicuous by its absence in amateur ensemble playing, is emphasized throughout.

Many teachers do the thinking for their pupils, instead of helping them to think for themselves. Insisting upon the mastery of each point will not dull their interest.

What greater gratification can there be for a pupil, whether he be a child or adult, than for him to recognize his increasing achievement.

Lessons marked "Supplementary Material" may be given as a reward for well-prepared work.

Class teaching should be a combination of individual instruction and ensemble playing. At every lesson there should be individual playing so that all the necessary corrections can be made. Never allow a pupil's mistakes to go unnoticed, since only in constant correction will he develop the habit of careful thinking and playing.

A decided advantage of group-teaching is that it provides experience in ensemble playing and gives every pupil the opportunity of listening to the others, of observing their mistakes, and of hearing the corrections.

Classes should be regraded whenever necessary so as not to retard the progress of the brighter students, nor to discourage the slower ones. This procedure also acts as an incentive for greater effort on the part of the pupils.

Lessons marked "Fingering", "Scales and Arpeggios", and "Important Assignment" should be used whenever necessary, according to the individual student's requirements.

The tests, following each five lessons, are given as a definite check on the pupil's progress of knowledge and accomplishment. These tests are most important and should not be omitted.

The eventual success of each pupil depends on the regular and careful home practice, according to directions.

If possible, it would be well for the teacher to keep in touch with the parents.

This course provides one lesson a week for a school year.

C. PAUL HERFURTH
HUGH M. STUART

RUDIMENTS OF MUSIC

Music is represented on paper by a combination of characters and signs; it is necessary to learn all of these in order to play the flute intelligently.

Characters called notes are written upon and between five lines, ===== called the staff.

The character 𝄞 placed at the beginning of the staff is called the treble or G clef.

The staff is divided by bars into measures as follows:

These measures, in turn, are equal in time value, according to the fractional numbers (Time signature) placed at the beginning of each piece.

The time signature indicates the number of notes of equal value in each measure. The upper figure gives the number of beats or counts in a measure, and the lower figure indicates what kind of a note has one beat, such as $\frac{4}{4}$ or $\mathbf{C}$ equals

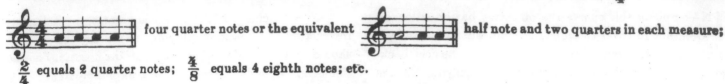

four quarter notes or the equivalent half note and two quarters in each measure; $\frac{2}{4}$ equals 2 quarter notes; $\frac{4}{8}$ equals 4 eighth notes; etc.

There are different kinds of notes, each variety representing a certain time value as follows:

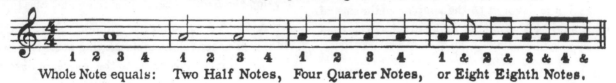

Whole Note equals: Two Half Notes, Four Quarter Notes, or Eight Eighth Notes.

The count for the above would be: four to the whole note: two to each half note: one to each quarter note, and one to each group of two eighth notes.

The notes are named after the first seven letters of the alphabet, i.e., a, b, c, d, e, f, g, according to the line on, or space in which they are placed.

The G clef which encircles the second line, establishes the note G on this line, from which the other lines and spaces are named as follows:

In addition notes are written upon and between short lines above and below the staff. These lines are called ledger lines.

A rest indicates a pause or silence for the value of the note after which it is named, such as

WHOLE REST   HALF RESTS   QUARTER RESTS   EIGHTH RESTS

The end of the piece is indicated by a light and heavy line:

When a section or part of a piece is to be repeated it will be shown by a double bar with two dots:

B. M. Co. 11832.

FOREWORD TO STUDENTS

No student should attempt the study of an instrument without the aid of a competent instructor for that particular instrument.

Due to the variations of mouth, teeth, and lip formations of different individuals, I believe the all important questions as to position of mouthpiece, breathing, tongueing, and lip control should be decided by your teacher for your particular case.

TECHNICS

The most important technics for wind instrument players are as follows:

(1) Developing and strengthening the lip muscles.
(Process)   Playing of long sustained tones.

(2) Developing clarity and precision in attacks.
(Process)   Proper use of the tongue.

(3) Developing a fine quality of tone.
(Process)   A combination of No. 1 and careful listening.

(4) Developing fluency in fingering.
(Process)   Playing of scales and arpeggios in various keys.

(5) Developing a mastery of the entire range of the instrument.
(Process)   A combination of all of the above.

Left Hand Thumb Position

CORRECT POSITION (POSTURE)

When playing the flute always stand or sit erect with head up. Arms, hands, and fingers should be completely relaxed and held in a natural position. Any stiffness of the body will be reflected in the quality of your playing. Fig. 1. When practicing, it is better to play in a standing position as this will help you to breathe properly.

HOLDING AND FINGERING THE FLUTE

The flute is balanced and supported by the first joint of the RIGHT thumb, which should press against the under side of the flute directly beneath the second finger of the RIGHT hand. The palm should be turned away from the player and the little finger should press key RC. The first finger of the LEFT hand, while curved to press key R1, should be pressed firmly at its first phalanx against the body of the flute. The palm should be toward the player. After these fingers are in place, the remaining fingers should fall into place easily if curved slightly.

CARE OF THE INSTRUMENT

Be sure to ask your teacher about caring for your instrument. A well cared-for instrument will play more easily.

PHRASING

The breathing marks ('), in addition to indicating the proper places to breathe, also serve as an introduction to the feeling of proper phrasing of melodies. This is important as it is that which gives meaning to music.

HOW TO PRACTICE

The most important part of your practicing is in being able to think out the problems at hand: fingering, tongueing, phrasing, etc. WHAT YOU CAN'T THINK YOU CAN'T PLAY. Be sure to do a good piece of work on lesson 1 before attempting lesson 2, and so on with each succeeding lesson. Play slowly at first and think carefully the rhythm (note values), phrasing, tone, fingering, and attack (tongueing). YOU are your own best teacher. Learn to intelligently criticise your own playing. I believe you know when you have done a good job and when you haven't. Don't be satisfied with a lesson half done, you are only fooling yourself. A good student is one who practices regularly every day. DO YOU?

DIAGRAM OF FINGERING

EMBOUCHURE HOLE

HEAD JOINT

MIDDLE JOINT

FOOT JOINT

LEFT HAND

RIGHT HAND

R·A
R·B
R·C·
R·D·
R·E·

	C	C#	Db	D	D#	Eb	E	F	F#	Gb	G	G#	Ab	A	A#	Bb	B	C	C#	Db	D	D
LEFT HAND THUMB																		(NO THUMB)	(NO THUMB)			
	T1	T1	T1	T1	T1	T1	T1	T1		T1	T1	T1		T1	T1	T1-2	T1				T1	T1
FIRST FINGER	1	1	1	1	1	1	1	1	1	1	1	1	1	1	1							
SECOND FINGER	2	2	2	2	2	2	2	2	2		2										2	2
THIRD FINGER	3	3	3	3	3	3		3	3	3											3	3
LEFT HAND FOURTH OR LITTLE FINGER — LX																						
RIGHT HAND FIRST FINGER	1	1	1	1	1	1								1							1	
SECOND FINGER	2	2	2	2	2																2	
THIRD FINGER	3	3	3	3			3														3	
RIGHT HAND FOURTH OR LITTLE FINGER	RD RE	RD		RC	RC	RC	RC		RC	RC		RC	RC	RC	RC	RC	RC	RC			RC	

L. MEANS LEFT HAND
R. MEANS RIGHT HAND

Note: If flute has open G# key, LX must be held down at all times unless G# or Ab are to be played.

B.M.Co. 11832 - 2

Take the head piece of the flute in your hands, with the open end to the right. Close the lips and extend the corners of the mouth slightly as when smiling. Place the inner edge of the hole against your lower lip so that the rim of the hole can be felt on the red part of the lip, just above the white. Be sure the hole is at the center of the lip. Place the tip of the tongue at the upper edge of the upper teeth. Take a good breath, withdraw the tongue slightly, and direct the air in a steady stream against the outer edge of the hole. The opening between the lips should be quite small in order to direct the stream of air against the rim of the hole without waste of air. (See picture below.)

Experiment with the position of the head piece against the lips; turn the hole slightly in or out, covering a little more or less of the hole. Listen to yourself. A better tone will be your guide.

When you can produce a tone and sustain it for the duration of your breath, try the following exercises for the head piece, Lesson One.

A TUNE A DAY

LESSON 1

OBJECTIVES:
1. To produce a tone on the head piece.
2. Correct position of the lips against the embouchure hole.
3. Correct use of the tongue.
4. Breathing, and the production of tone.
5. To learn the value of whole, half, and quarter notes and rests.
6. To learn a meter (time) signature and what it does.

METER (time) SIGNATURE. $\frac{4}{4}$ MEANS { Four counts to a measure. / A quarter note gets one count.

Exercises for Head Piece

Practice these exercises many times and devote a considerable amount of your practice time playing long tones in front of a mirror where you can see the position of your lips.

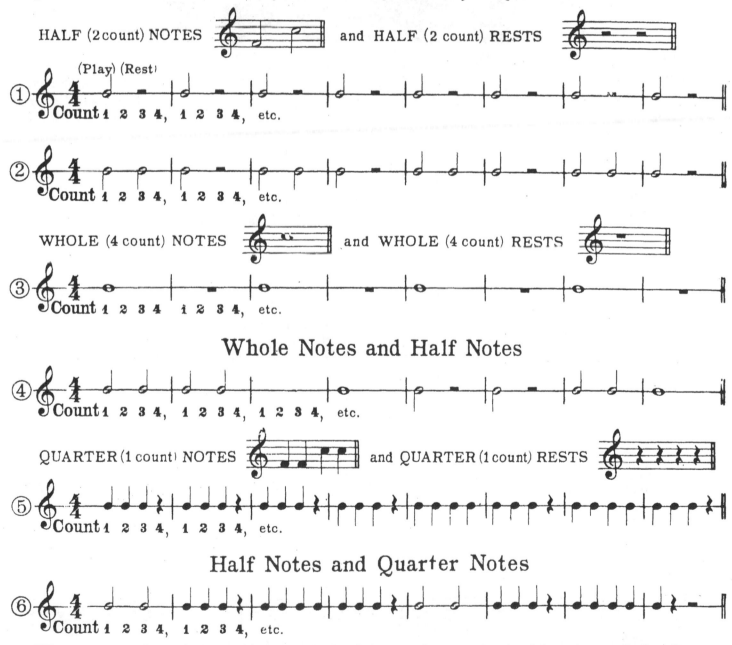

When you can play a full round tone on the headpiece, and you understand how to count the above exercises, your teacher will show you how to assemble the flute and you will be ready to proceed to LESSON 1A.

B.M.Co. 11832

LESSON 1A

OBJECTIVES: 1. Correct posture and correct holding of flute.
2. Further development of mouth position.
3. To introduce third-line B.

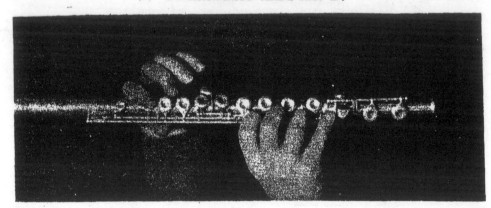

LEFT HAND

First finger on key 1;
Thumb on key T1;
First finger against flute
at first phalanx.

RIGHT HAND

Thumb beneath flute
under second finger;
Little finger on key RC.

Introducing 3rd-line B
T1 (L1) (Key RC)

FINGERING GUIDE
LEFT HAND 1 2 3 (●) Means key pressed down.
RIGHT HAND 1 2 3 (○) Means key open.

① This note is ___ ?   ② Play slowly   REPEAT
Think: Count 1 2 3 4   REPEAT

③ ④ These are ___ notes and receive ___ counts?
Think: Count 1 2 3 4

⑤ These are ___ notes?   ⑥
Think: Count 1 2 3 4   1 2 3 4 1 2 3 4

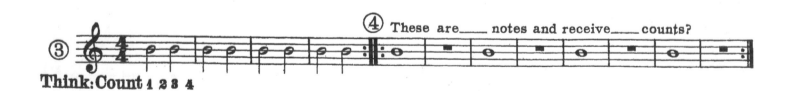

B.M. Co. 11832

LESSON 1B

OBJECTIVES: 1. Correct position and correct holding of flute.
2. To introduce second-space A.

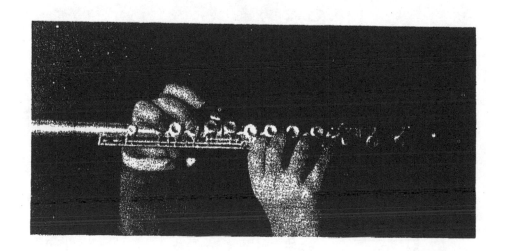

Introducing 2nd-space A
T1 (L1-2) (Key RC)

Play slowly

② This note is ___?

① Think: Count 1 2 3 4   1 2 3 4

These are ___ notes and receive ___ counts? ④

③ Think: Count 1 2 3 4   1234   1234

B and A March
(Duet)

C. P. H.

⑤ Pupil

Think: Count 1 2 3 4   1 2 3 4

Teacher

B.M.Co. 11832

LESSON 1B (continued)

OBJECTIVES: 1. To introduce second-line G.
2. Practical application of previous knowledge.

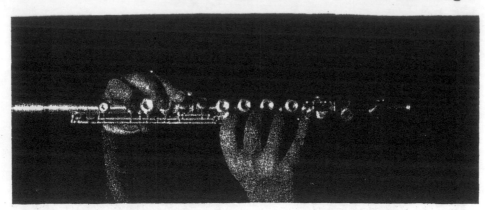

Introducing 2nd-line G
T1 (L1-2-3) (Key RC)

This note is ___?

⑦ Play slowly

⑥ Think:Count 1 2 3 4

⑧ Think:Count 1 2 3 4 1 2 3 4

⑨ These notes are ___ notes?

1 2 3 4

These are ___ notes and recieve ___ counts? ⑪

⑩ Think:Count 1 2 3 4

1 2 3 4

⑫ Think:Count 1   2   3   4

Merrily
(Duet)

⑬ Pupil

Think:Count 1 2 3 4

*)

Teacher

Hold each note as long as possible.

⑭

*When two notes on the same degree (line or space) of the staff are connected by a curved line ⌒ they are to be played as one note, adding the value of the two notes together. This is called a TIE.
**Hold (fermata): a short curved line drawn over a dot, lengthens the value of the note.

B.M.Co. 11832

LESSON 2

OBJECTIVES:
1. To develop a fuller tone.
2. Practice in the use of whole, half, and quarter notes and rests.
3. Application of pre-knowledge.

Hold each note as long as possible.

The Swing — H.M.S.

Ten Pins — H.M.S.

Flying Fancies — H.M.S.

In a Canoe — H.M.S.

The Bells (Duet) — H.M.S.

At Pierrot's Door (Duet) — French Folk Song

Long Tones

Home work: Write a line of notes thus far studied, using half and quarter notes and rests.
Mark the letter name (G-A-B) above each note.

B.M.Co. 11832

LESSON 3

OBJECTIVES: 1. To learn the name and fingering for third-space C.
2. Continuation of previous objectives.

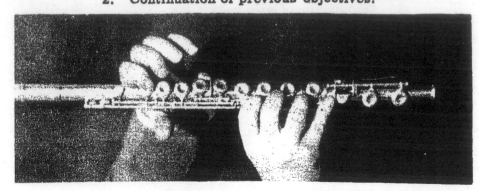

LESSON 3A

OBJECTIVE: Application of pre-knowledge.

Happy Days
(Duet)

B. P. S.

Kassaksavell
(Duet)

H. M. S.

Folk-Song
(Duet)

Melody
(Duet)

Hold each note as long as possible.

Home work: Write a line of notes thus far studied, marking the name of each.

B.M.Co. 11882

LESSON 4

OBJECTIVES: 1. To learn the name and fingering for first-space F.
2. To develop a clearer tone by playing long tones.
3. Emphasis on rhythm.

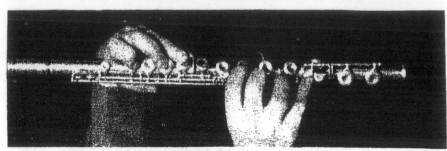

Introducing 1st-space F
T1 (L1-2-3) (R1) Key RC

Think: Count 1 2 3 4

② This note is ___?

Think: Count 1 2 3 4

④ These are ___ notes?

Think: Count 1 2 3 4

Hold each note as long as possible.

Different Note Values

Ⓐ The letter name of this note is ___?
Ⓑ This note is ___?
Ⓒ This note is ___?

Ⓓ This note is ___?
Ⓔ This note is ___?

Folk-Song
(Duet)

French

Time signature is ___?

Pupil

1 2 3 4

Teacher

Home work: Write a line of notes thus far learned, using half and quarter notes and marking the letter names above the notes.

B.M.Co. 11832

LESSON 5

OBJECTIVES: 1 To learn the name and fingering for third-line B-flat.
2. To learn the meaning of the flat (♭).
3. To notice key signatures and learn what they mean.

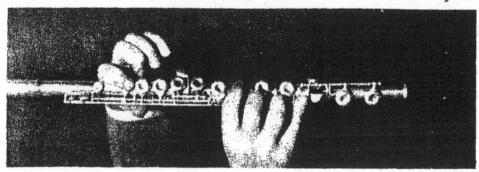

Introducing 3rd-line B-flat
T1 (L1) (R1) Key RC

A FLAT (♭) LOWERS THE NOTE TO WHICH IT APPLIES BY ONE HALF TONE. A NATURAL (♮) TAKES AWAY THE EFFECT OF A SHARP* OR FLAT AND RESTORES THE NOTE TO ITS ORIGINAL PITCH. (*see Lesson Nine)

The Key of F Major

The flat (♭) placed on the 3rd line of the staff just after the clef sign, affects every B throughout the piece, except when temporarily cancelled by a natural (♮) sign. NOTICE KEY SIGNATURES, AND FINGER ACCORDINGLY.

AN ACCIDENTAL IS A SHARP OR FLAT WHICH DOES NOT BELONG TO THE KEY SIGNATURE AND APPLIES ONLY TO THE MEASURE IN WHICH IT IS PLACED.

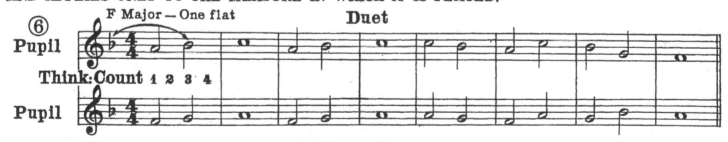

Oats and Beans
(Duet)

B.M.Co. 11522

LESSON 5A

OBJECTIVES: 1. To introduce the slur.
2. To practice using the notes previously learned.
3. Further use of the key of F.

This sign ⌒ when placed over or below two or more notes, indicates that they are to be played in one breath, and that only the first note in each group should be tongued.

Lightly Row

German Folk-Song

Jingle Bells

J. Pierpont

B.M.Co. 11832

TEST QUESTIONS THROUGH LESSON 5A

Questions from this and following test-sheets will be given as a check on your home study of the preceding lessons.

REMEMBER: The more you know and understand about the signs and symbols used in music-writing, the easier it will be for you to learn to play well.

	Points	Your score
1. This ⎯⎯⎯⎯ is called⎯⎯⎯⎯⎯.	5	....
2. This symbol 𝄞 is called⎯⎯⎯⎯⎯⎯.	5	....
3. The staff is divided by bar-lines into⎯⎯⎯⎯⎯⎯.	5	....
4. Fractions at the beginning of music are called ⎯⎯⎯⎯⎯ signatures.	5	....
5. This 𝄞 is a⎯⎯⎯ note and has ⎯⎯⎯ counts.	4	....
6. These 𝄞 are ⎯⎯⎯ notes and have⎯⎯⎯ counts each.	4	....
7. These 𝄞 are⎯⎯⎯ notes and have ⎯⎯⎯ count each.	4	....
8. Lines and spaces are named after the first ⎯⎯⎯ letters of the alphabet.	5	....
9. This 𝄞 is a ⎯⎯⎯ rest.	4	....
10. These 𝄞 are ⎯⎯⎯ rests.	4	....
11. These 𝄞 are⎯⎯⎯ rests.	4	....
12. This sign 𝄞 means⎯⎯⎯ counts to each measure.	5	....
13. Name the notes thus far studied:⎯⎯⎯⎯⎯⎯⎯⎯⎯⎯⎯⎯⎯	6	....
14. Write (notate) the notes thus far studied:	6	....
15. Write the letter names above the following notes.	6	....

| 16. Divide the following into measures. | 6 | .... |

17. Inspection of instrument.	10	....
18. Sight reading.	12	....
	100	

TEACHER: Write line of notes thus far studied, using whole, half, and quarter notes as a sight reading test.

B.M.Co. 11832

LESSON 6

OBJECTIVES: 1. To learn the name and fingering for fourth-line D.
2. Practice in changing registers through C, B, and A.

Introducing 4th-line D
T1 (L 2-3) (R 1-2-3)

Play slowly

① Think:Count 1 2 3 4

③ Think:Count 1 2 3 4

⑤ *Keep fingers close to keys* 5A
Think:Count 1 2 3 4

⑥ *Practice silently first*
Think:Count 1 2 3 4

⑦ Think:Count 1 2 3 4

Upidee (One flat: B♭)
(Duet)

⑧ Pupil
THINK
Think:Count 1 2 3 4
THINK
Pupil

Upidee (No sharps or flats)
(Duet)

⑨ Pupil
Think:Count 1 2 3 4
Pupil

*Silent Practice on page 13 may be introduced here if desired.
B.M.Co. 11832

OBJECTIVES: 1. To attain more facility in changing registers.
.2. Application of pre-knowledge.

Silent Practice

In a sitting position rest the flute comfortably with mouthpiece on the left shoulder, the opposite end on your lap, and practice the register change from C to D or B to D many times until you can do it easily and reasonably rapidly.

LESSON 7

OBJECTIVES:
1. To learn the name and fingering for first-line E.
2. To learn the name and fingering for fourth-space E.
3. Practical application of these notes.

Introducing 1st-line E
T1 (L1-2-3) (R1-2) Key RC

Introducing 4th-space E
T1 (L1-2-3) (R1-2) Key RC

① This note is ___ ?
Think: Count 1 2 3 4

② This note is ___ ?

③ Think: Count 1 2 3 4

④

⑤ Key of ___ ?
Think: Count 1 2 3 4

⑥ Key of ___ ?

Melody
THINK   Hymn
⑦ Think: Count 1 2 3 4

Abide with Me
W. H. Monk
THINK
⑧ Think: Count 1 2 3 4

Folk-Song
(Duet)

⑨ Pupil
Think: Count 1 2 3 4

Teacher

LESSON 8

OBJECTIVES: 1. To learn the name and fingering for fifth-line F.
2. Further practice using notes previously learned.
3. Further use of the key of F.

Introducing 5th-line F
T1 (L1-2-3) (R1) Key RC

See picture on page 8.

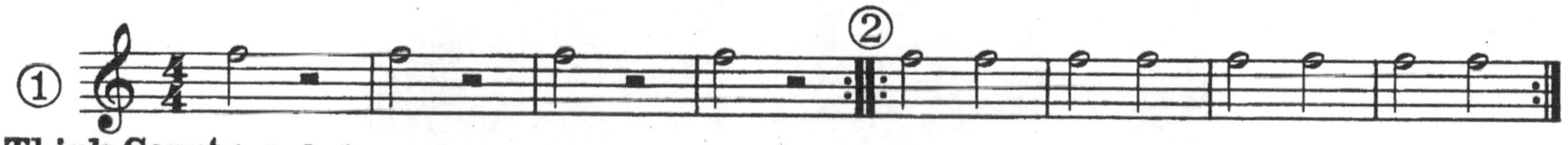

① Think:Count 1 2 3 4

③ Think:Count 1 2 3 4

Hold each note as long as possible.

⑤

Scale of F Major

⑥ Think:Count 1 2 3 4

Up and Down

Trauts

⑦ Think:Count 1 2 3 4

Song of the Volga Boatmen

Folk-Song

Slowly

⑧ Think:Count 1 2 3 4

Evening Song

Robert Schumann

Slowly

⑨ Think:Count 1 2 3 4

B.M.Co. 11832

LESSON 9

OBJECTIVES:
1. To learn the name and fingering for first-space F-sharp.
2. To learn the name and fingering for fifth-line F-sharp.
3. To learn the meaning of the sharp (♯).
4. Practical application of these notes

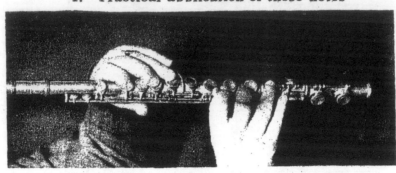

Introducing 1st-space F♯
T1 (L1-2-3) (R3) Key RC

Introducing 5th-line F♯
T1 (L1-2-3) (R3) Key RC

A SHARP (♯) RAISES THE NOTE TO WHICH IT APPLIES BY ONE HALF STEP.

This note is ___?

② ③ ④ ⑤

Au Clair de la Lune

This mark (؍) indicates the breathing places.

Lully

⑥ Think: Count 1 2 3 4

Merrily We Roll Along

⑦ Think: Count 1 2 3 4

Folk-Song

German

⑧ Think: Count 1 2 3 4

Melody

C. P. H.

⑨ Think: Count 1 2 3 4

Home work: Write a line of the notes thus far studied.

B.M.Co. 11832

LESSON 10

OBJECTIVES:
1. To learn the name and fingering for G, first space above the staff.
2. To introduce the key of G, one sharp.
3. Application of pre-knowledge.

Introducing G,
1st space above the staff
T1 (L1-2-3) Key RC

See picture page 4.

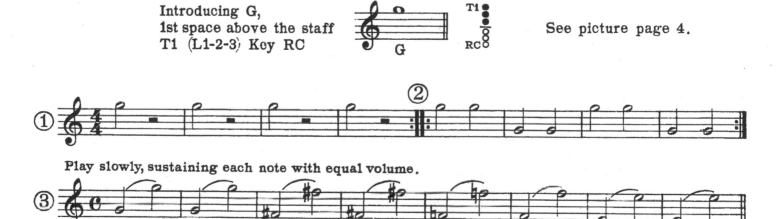

Play slowly, sustaining each note with equal volume.

The Key of G Major

The sharp (♯) placed on the top line of the staff, just after the clef sign, affects every F throughout the piece, except when temporarily cancelled by a natural (♮) sign.
NOTICE KEY SIGNATURES, AND FINGER ACCORDINGLY.

Scale of G Major

Beneath Thy Guiding Hand

J. Hatton

Think: Count 1 2 3 4

THINK

Theme from the Second Symphony

F. J. Haydn

Key of___?

Think: Count 1 2 3 4

B.M.Co. 11332

TEST QUESTIONS THROUGH LESSON 10

		Points	Your score
1.	This :‖: means _____ .	4	....
2.	This (♭) is a _____ .	4	....
3.	How does a (♭) affect a note? _____	4	....
4.	This (♮) is a _____ .	4	....
5.	How does a (♮) affect a note? _____	4	....
6.	Name the following lines and spaces of the staff:	8	....

    1st space _____   2nd space _____
    3rd space _____   1st line   _____
    3rd line   _____   2nd line   _____
    4th space _____   1st space below staff _____

		Points	Your score
7.	The key of (1♭) is _____ .	4	....
8.	Write (notate) the key signature of (1♭).	4	....
9.	This sign ⌒ connecting two notes of the same pitch is called? _____ .	4	....
10.	What is a slur? _____ .	6	....
11.	Write (notate) the G major scale.	8	....
12.	The key of (1♯) is _____ .	4	....
13.	Notate the key signature of (1♯).	4	....
14.	This note is _____ .	4	....
15.	This note is _____ .	4	....
16.	This note is _____ .	4	....
17.	Music written for two flutes is called _____ .	6	....
18.	Inspection of instrument.	10	....
19.	Sight reading.	<u>10</u> 100	....

TEACHER: Write line of notes thus far studied, using slurs.

B.M.Co. 11832

LESSON 11

OBJECTIVES: 1. To learn the name and fingering for A, first line above the staff.
2. To learn the value of the eighth note.
3. To learn the use of rhythms involving 8th notes in $\frac{4}{4}$ and $\frac{2}{4}$ time.
4. To learn the meaning of *D.S. (Dal Segno).*

Introducing A,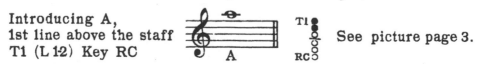
1st line above the staff
T1 (L 12) Key RC   See picture page 3.

Eighth Notes

An eighth note (♪) is equal to one half the value of a quarter note. Two eighth notes (♫) equal one quarter note, four eighth notes (♫♫) a half note, and eight eighths (♫♫ ♫♫) a whole note. An eighth rest (✷) is equal to the value of an eighth note.

$\frac{2}{4}$ TIME MEANS ⎰Two counts to a measure.
⎱A quarter note gets one count.

D.S.-(Dal Segno) = go back to this sign ✗ and play to *Fine* (End).

B.M.Co. 11832

LESSON 12

OBJECTIVES: 1. To learn the names and fingerings for B and C above the staff.
2. Further practice using eighth notes.
3. Further practice using $\frac{2}{4}$ time.

Scale of C Major

Slurred Octaves

Andante
from the Surprise Symphony

F. J. Haydn

Reuben and Rachel

Allegretto (briskly)

Minka

Moderato (moderately)

Wearing of the Green

Irish Air

Allegro (with spirit)

Old MacDonald
(Duet)

Allegretto

Pupil

Count 1 & 2 &

Pupil

Home work: Learn to play the C Major scale from memory.

B.M.Co. 11832

SUPPLEMENTARY MATERIAL THROUGH LESSON 12

There's Music in the Air

*Many pieces begin with an incomplete measure, usually starting with the last beat or fraction thereof. This is called an up-beat. The ending always completes the measure of the up-beat.

B.M.Co. 11832

LESSON 13

OBJECTIVES: 1. To learn a new time signature – $\frac{3}{4}$ time – with emphasis on rhythm drills (A–B–C, etc.)
2. To learn the value and use of dotted quarter and dotted half notes.

The Dotted Half Note and the Dotted Quarter Note

A dot is equal to one half the value of the note it follows. A dotted half note equals 3 beats, a dotted quarter note equals $1\frac{1}{2}$ beats.

Rhythm Drills

DRILL: Count aloud each variation while clapping hands once for each note. Repeat several times until you feel the rhythm before playing. Variation F is the most difficult and should be thoroughly understood.

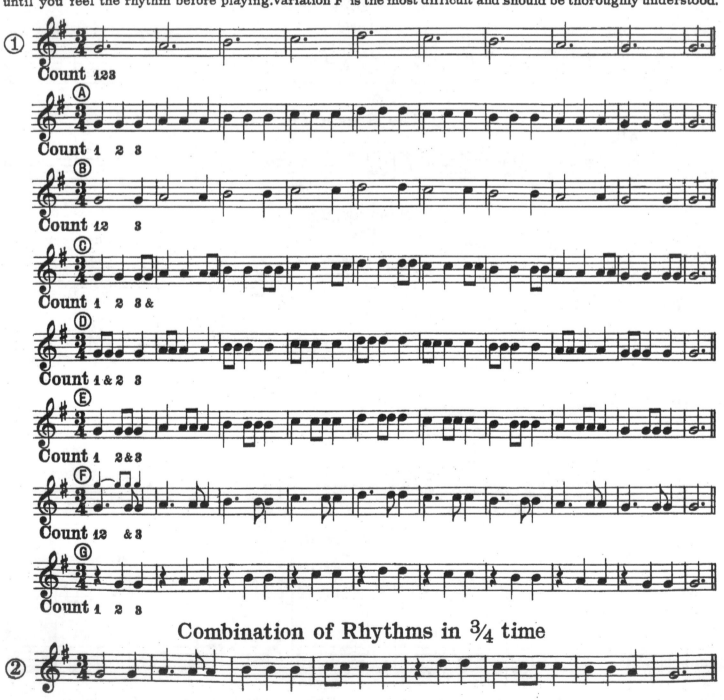

Combination of Rhythms in ¾ time

LESSON 14

OBJECTIVE: Application of $\frac{2}{4}$ and $\frac{3}{4}$ rhythms in familiar melodies of different keys.

French Folk-Song

Home work: Write eight measures of notes thus far studied, using different rhythms in $\frac{3}{4}$ time. Mark beats and name notes.

B.M.Co. 11832

LESSON 15

OBJECTIVES: 1. To learn the name and fingering for B-flat above the staff.
2. Application of pre-knowledge by playing familiar melodies.

Go Down Moses
Negro Spiritual

Think: Count 4 1 2 3 4

1 2 3 4

Melody in F
(Adapted)
A. Rubinstein

The time signature is ___?

THINK

Think: Count 1 2 &

Yankee Doodle
Traditional

Think: Count 1 & 2 &

Folk-Song

UP-BEAT

Think: Count 3 & 1 2 3

Crusader's Hymn
German

Think: Count 1 2 3 4

Don't forget to play long tones regularly.

*This fingering for B♭ is used primarily when B♭ is approached from G.

B.M.Co. 11832

TEST QUESTIONS THROUGH LESSON 15

		Points	Your score
1.	These 🎵 are _____ notes.	5	....
2.	Each of the above notes receives _____ count in $\frac{4}{4}$ or $\frac{2}{4}$ time.	5	....
3.	This 🎵 is a _____ note.	5	....
4.	The above note has _____ counts.	5	....
5.	This 🎵 is a _____ note.	5	....
6.	The above note has _____ counts.	5	....
7.	Divide the following into measures:	5	....

🎵 (rhythm notation)

8.	Mark the count under the following:	10	....

🎵 (rhythm notation)

9.	This sign ⌒ means _____.	2	....
10.	What is meant by the up-beat? _____	5	....
11.	This (♮) is a _____.	2	....
12.	How does a ♮ affect a note? _____.	3	....
13.	The name of this note 🎵 is _____.	3	....
14.	The key of (1♯) is _____.	5	....
15.	Write (notate) the key signature of (1♯). 🎵	5	....
16.	What is the meaning of *D. S. (Dal Segno)?* _____	5	....
17.	What is the meaning of $\frac{2}{4}$ time? _____	5	....
18.	What is an accidental? _____	5	....
19.	What is the meaning of Andante? _____ Allegretto? _____	5	....
20.	Sight reading.	$\frac{10}{100}$	....

🎵 (blank staff)

TEACHER: Write line of notes using different rhythm patterns in $\frac{3}{4}$ time.

B.M.Co. 11832

LESSON 16

OBJECTIVES:
1. To learn the name and fingering for low D.
2. Knowledge of first and second endings.
3. Practice in playing in the low register.

Introducing D,
1st space below the staff
T1 (L1-2-3) (R1-2-3)

Folk-Song

Au Clair de la Lune

Key of _____. Sharps are _____, and _____.   Lully (?)

First and Second Ending

The term 1st and 2nd ending applies to one or more measures in brackets at a double bar: ⌐1.   ⌐2.   .Thus, when the strain is repeated, the first ending is omitted and the second ending played instead.

Home on the Range

Cowboy Song

⑤ Time signature is _____? (9)   1. First ending

Think: Count 3   1 2 3   12 & 3   12 3&

2. Second ending

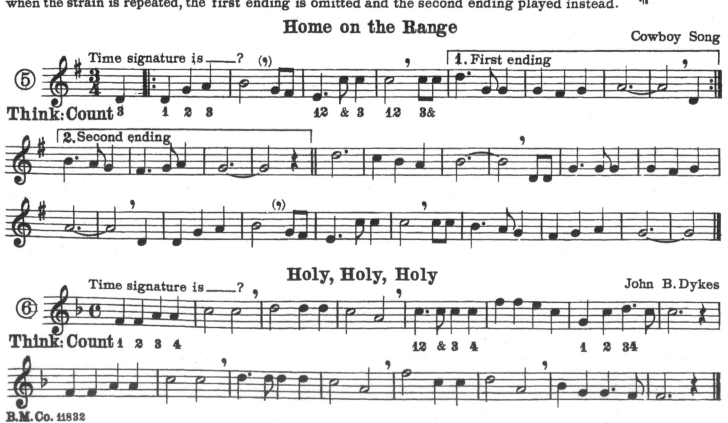

Holy, Holy, Holy

John B. Dykes

⑥ Time signature is _____?

Think: Count 1 2 3 4   12 & 3 4   1 2 34

B.M.Co. 11832

LESSON 17

OBJECTIVES:
1. To learn the name and fingering for third-space C-sharp.
2. To learn the name and fingering for C-sharp above the staff.
3. To learn the meaning of the key of D Major.

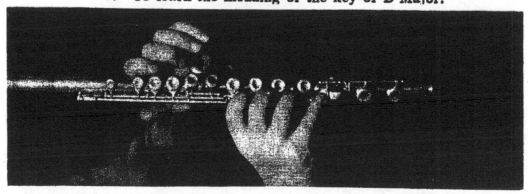

Introducing 3rd-space C#.
Key RC (no other fingers)

No fingers
Key RC

Introducing C#,
2nd line above the staff.
Key RC

(Same as lower C#)

Key of D Major
Two sharps: F# and C#

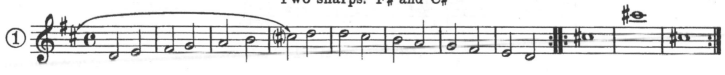

Hymn
F. J. Haydn

Think: Count 4   123 4

Harvest Time
C.P.H.

Key of _____ . Sharps are _____ .

Holy, Holy, Holy
John B. Dykes

THINK

Duet
Carl M. von Weber

Andante

Pupil

Think key and note values.

Pupil

B.M. Co. 11832

LESSON 18

OBJECTIVES: 1. To review the keys and fingerings presented in previous lessons.
2. To review the various rhythms presented in previous lessons.
3. Further practice of long tones and slurred octaves.

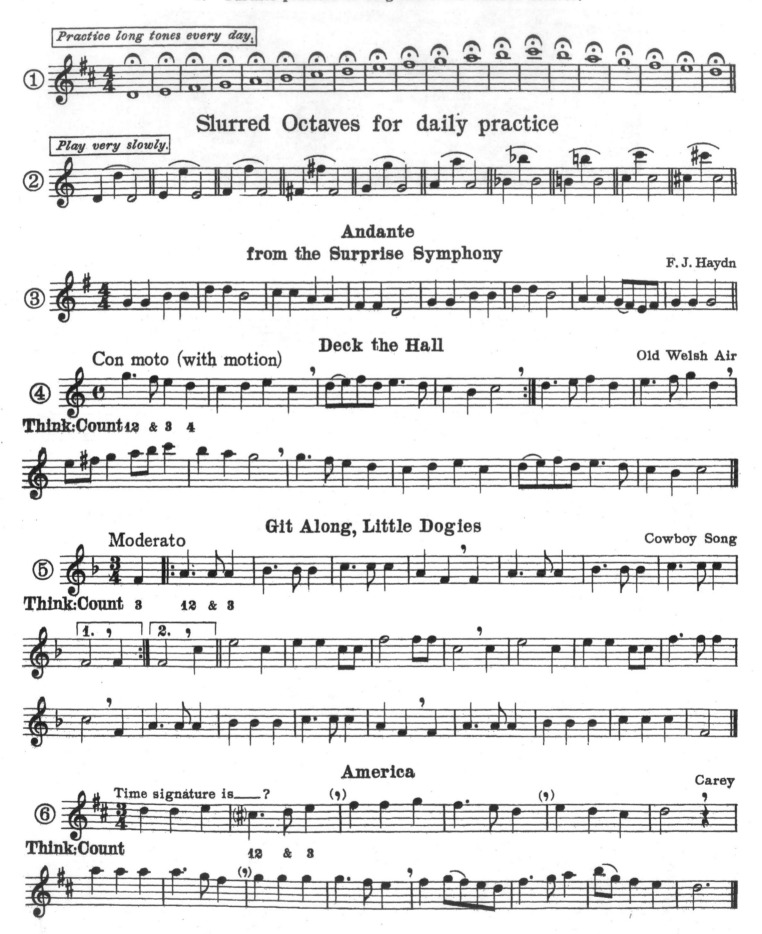

Practice long tones every day.

Slurred Octaves for daily practice

Play very slowly.

Andante
from the Surprise Symphony
F. J. Haydn

Deck the Hall
Old Welsh Air

Con moto (with motion)

Think:Count 1 2 & 3 4

Git Along, Little Dogies
Cowboy Song

Moderato

Think:Count 3 1 2 & 3

America
Carey

Time signature is____?

Think:Count 1 2 & 3

LESSON 19

OBJECTIVES:
1. To learn the name and fingering for fourth-space E-flat.
2. To learn the name and fingering for first-line E-flat.
3. To learn the meaning of the key of B-flat Major.
4. To play familiar melodies in the key of B flat Major.

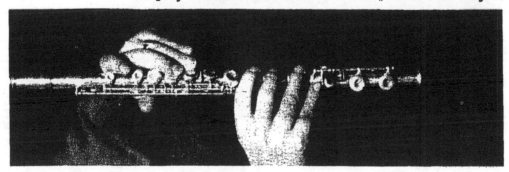

Introducing 4th-space Eb
T1 (L2-3) (R1-2-3) Key RC

Introducing 1st-line Eb
T1 (L1-2-3) (R1-2-3) Key RC

Key of Bb Major
Two flats: Bb and Eb

Hymn

Time signature is ___?

Think: Count 1 2 3

The Merry Widow Waltz

Lehár

Key of__; flats are__ & __.
Tempo di Valse (in waltz time)

Think: Count 1 2 3

How Can I Leave Thee

F. Kücken

Think: Count 1 2 3 4

B.M. Co. 11832

SUPPLEMENTARY MATERIAL—LESSONS 13 TO 19

Massa's in the Cold, Cold Ground
(Duet)

S. Foster

The Blue Bells of Scotland
(Duet)

Old Scotch Air

Auld Lang Syne
(Duet)

Scotch Air

TEST QUESTIONS THROUGH LESSON 19

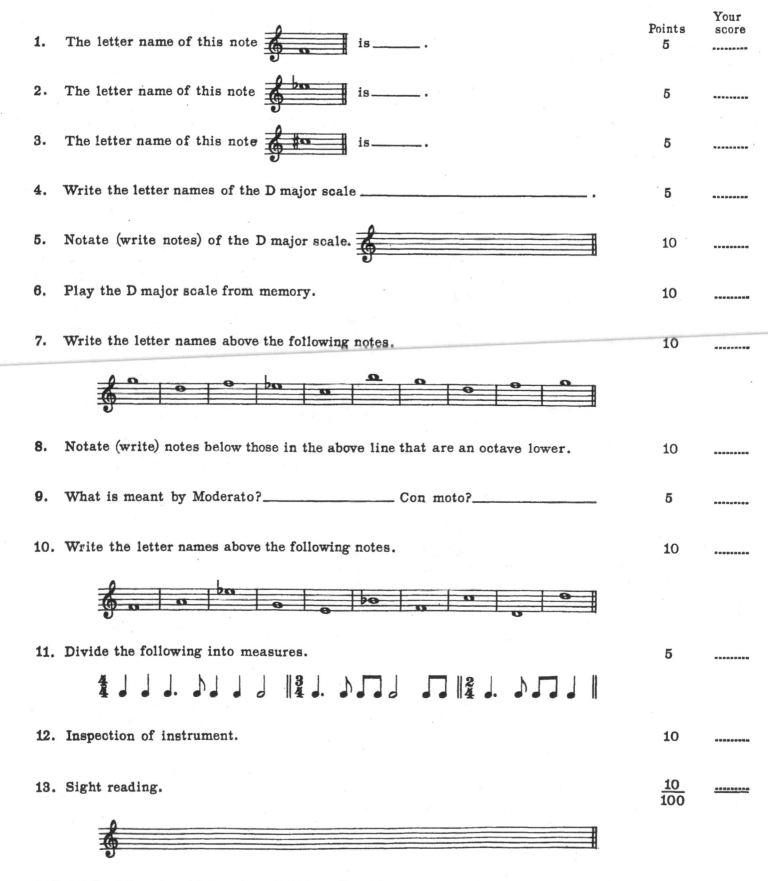

		Points	Your score
1.	The letter name of this note ___ is ___ .	5	--------
2.	The letter name of this note ___ is ___ .	5	--------
3.	The letter name of this note ___ is ___ .	5	--------
4.	Write the letter names of the D major scale ___ .	5	--------
5.	Notate (write notes) of the D major scale. ___	10	--------
6.	Play the D major scale from memory.	10	--------
7.	Write the letter names above the following notes.	10	--------
8.	Notate (write) notes below those in the above line that are an octave lower.	10	--------
9.	What is meant by Moderato? ___ Con moto? ___	5	--------
10.	Write the letter names above the following notes.	10	--------
11.	Divide the following into measures.	5	--------
12.	Inspection of instrument.	10	--------
13.	Sight reading.	10 / 100	--------

TEACHER: Write line of notes using both registers.

B.M.Co. 11832

LESSON 20

OBJECTIVES: 1. To learn a new rhythm.
2. To understand *Alla breve* (cut time) ($\frac{2}{2}$ time).

Comparison of ¢ with $\frac{2}{4}$ time

Alla breve ($\frac{2}{2}$) or cut time (¢) is played the same as $\frac{2}{4}$ time. Each note has half the value as in $\frac{4}{4}$ time, a half note being the unit of a beat.

Rhythm Drills

Drill: Count aloud each pattern while clapping hands once for each note.
   REMEMBER-Unless you feel the rhythm you cannot play it.
Play the C scale, using these patterns until the rhythms are memorized.

There's Music in the Air*

Compare the measures of this song with ①,②,③,④ above.

G. Root

*Compare with the same song in $\frac{4}{4}$ time, Supplementary Exercises, page 21.

LESSON 21

OBJECTIVES: 1. Continuation of *Alla breve* (cut time).
2. To learn some new musical terms.
3. Application of pre-knowledge.

A Capital Ship

In march time (Tempo di Marcia)

Old English Tune

College Song*

Allegro (fast)

J. Brahms

Theme from "Rosamunde"

Allegro

F. Schubert

NEW MUSICAL TERMS

p - *piano* = softly.
mf - *mezzo forte* = medium loud.
f - *forte* = loudly
cresc. - *crescendo* = gradually louder.

rit. - *ritenuto* = gradually slower.
a tempo = the original speed.
⌒ - *fermata* = hold longer.
𝄎 = repeat the preceding measure.

*This theme (melody) was used by Brahms in his "Academic Festival Overture."

B.M.Co. 11832

LESSON 22

OBJECTIVE: Further practice using cut time.

Marines' Hymn

Official Song of the
U.S. Marine Corps

Tempo di Marcia

Caisson Song

Maj. E. L. Gruber

Tempo di Marcia

La Cinquantaine

Gabriel-Marie

Allegretto

Home work: Write a line of notes in cut time, marking beats and naming notes.

* —◁ gradually louder; ▷— gradually softer.

B.M.Co. 11832

LESSON 23

OBJECTIVES: 1. To learn another new rhythm.
2. Knowledge and use of the rhythm of $\frac{6}{8}$ time.
3. Counting 6 to a measure and 2 to a measure.
4. Application of new rhythm in familiar melodies.

Row, Row, Row your Boat

Folk-Song

Oats and Beans

Folk-Song

The Mulberry Bush

Folk-Song

Pop Goes the Weasel

Folk-Song

*Play slowly at first, counting six beats to each measure, and increase the speed as you are able, until fast enough to count two beats to each measure.

B.M.Co. 11832

LESSON 24

OBJECTIVES:
1. Continuation of six-eight time (slow).
2. Counting six beats to the measure.
3. Application of pre-knowledge in familiar tunes.
4. Playing a duet in six-eight time.

Barcarolle

D.C. (Da Capo) = go back to the beginning and play to Fine.

B.M.Co. 11833

LESSON 25

OBJECTIVES:
1. Continuation of six-eight time (fast).
2. Counting two beats to a measure (march time).
3. Application of previous knowledge in familiar tunes.

Funiculi-Funicula
(Duet)
Luigi Denza

Progress March
C.P.H.

* See page 33

B.M.Co. 11832

LESSON 26

OBJECTIVES: 1. To learn the name and fingering for A-flat.
2. To learn the name and fingering for G-sharp.
3. Knowledge of enharmonic tones.

ENHARMONIC TONES are notes that sound the same though given different names because they are written on different degrees of the staff.

Ab and G# are ENHARMONIC TONES

LESSON 27

OBJECTIVES: 1. To learn the use of sixteenth notes.
2. To learn to count sixteenth notes.

Sixteenth Notes

A sixteenth note (♬) is equal to one half the value of an eighth note (♪).

Two sixteenth notes equal one eighth note (♬ = ♪) and four sixteenth notes equal one quarter note (♬♬ = ♩).

Comparative table showing number of sixteenth notes to other notes studied thus far:

from A Midsummer Night's Dream

Mendelssohn

Listen to the Mocking Bird

Kingdom Comin'

Home work: Write a line of notes, using different groupings of sixteenth notes.
    Memorize "Folk-Song" (lesson 24, number 2)

B.M.Co. 11832

OBJECTIVES: 1. To introduce high D.
                    2. To learn the D Major scale (two octaves).
                    3. Practical application of the new note.

Introducing D, 3rd space above the staff
T1 (L 2-3) Key RC

Scale of D Major

Scale of D Major (two octaves)

Play slowly at first and gradually increase speed to that of eighth notes.

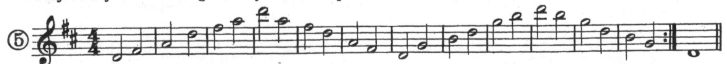

Home, Sweet Home
(Duet)

Bishop

Andante

Pupil

Pupil

Oh, Come all ye Faithful

J. Reading

Moderato

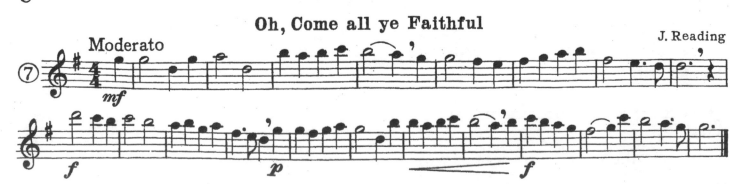

B.M.Co. 11832

OBJECTIVES: 1. To learn dotted eighth and sixteenth notes, *legato*.
2. To learn the correct division of each beat.
3. Application of new rhythm.

Dotted Eighth and Sixteenth Notes
Legato (Connected)

This is one of the more difficult rhythms to learn. The dotted eighth note is equal to three sixteenth notes. Always feel a division of four on each beat when playing this rhythm, three on the dotted eighth, and one on the sixteenth.

BE SURE TO PLAY THE DOTTED EIGHTH NOTE LONG ENOUGH AND THE SIXTEENTH NOTE SHORT ENOUGH.

Largo
from the "New World" Symphony
(Duet)

A. Dvořák

(see page 38)

dim. (diminuendo) = gradually softer.

B.M.Co. 11832

LESSON 30

OBJECTIVES: 1. To learn dotted eighth and sixteenth notes, *staccato*.
2. Application of this difficult rhythm in familiar melodies, using $\frac{2}{4}$ and $\frac{4}{4}$ time.

Dotted Eighth and Sixteenth Notes
Staccato (Detached)

Dotted eighth and sixteenth notes played *staccato* (detached) are separated by a short pause. Notice how these notes are written and how they are actually played.

Joy to the World
(Duet)

G. F. Handel

Battle Hymn of the Republic

Steffe

*A dot (.) above or below a note indicates that the note is to be played short. This is called *staccato*.

B.M.Co. 11832

OBJECTIVE: Continued application of dotted eighth and sixteenth notes in
$\frac{3}{4}$ and $\frac{6}{8}$ time.

Maryland, My Maryland
(Duet)

German Folk-Song

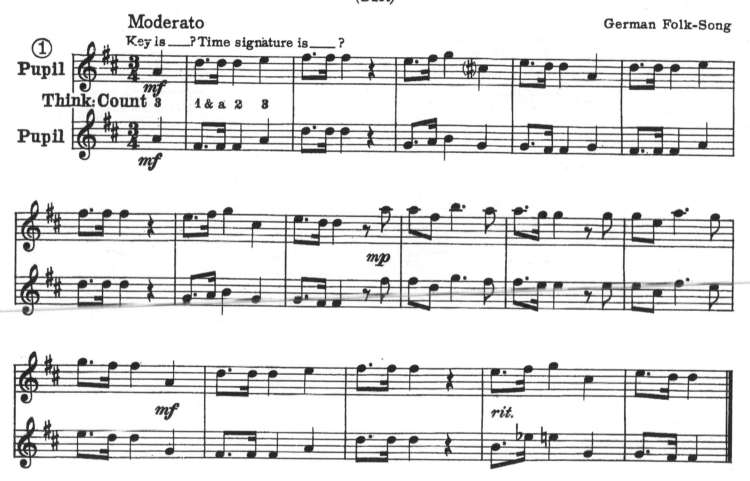

Silent Night, Holy Night
(Duet)

F. Gruber

B.M.Co. 11832

LESSON 32

OBJECTIVES:
1. To understand and play chromatics.
2. To learn more about enharmonic tones.
3. To learn new fingerings.

Chromatics

The word "chromatic" means moving by half steps. A chromatic scale is one that ascends or descends by half steps. Enharmonic tones sound the same even though they are notated on different degrees of the staff.

BE SURE TO LEARN THE PROPER NAMES AND FINGERINGS FOR BOTH ASCENDING AND DESCENDING CHROMATIC SCALES.

Chromatic Scale of C in Two Octaves

Play slowly at first, and gradually increase speed.

Chromatic Etude

Fr. Wohlfahrt

Triplets

Triplets are groups of three notes played in the time of two notes of the same value. They are indicated by a figure *3* and a slur placed over or under a group of three notes. A triplet of eighth notes is equal to two eighth notes or one quarter note.

A measure of $\frac{2}{4}$ containing two triplets is the same as a measure of $\frac{6}{8}$ in march time.

Triplet Etude

Moderato

Klose

*D♯ fingered like E♭

B.M.Co. 11832

SUPPLEMENTARY MATERIAL THROUGH LESSON 33

Santa Lucia

Andantino*

Neapolitan Boat Song

Country Gardens

Allegretto

Folk-Song

Dixie

Allegretto

D. Emmet

*Andantino - Not quite as slow as *Andante*.
**In three-eight time the eighth note is the unit of a beat (♪).

B.M. Co. 11832

TEST QUESTIONS THROUGH LESSON 33

		Points	Your score
1.	Notate (write) the upper octave of the C major scale.	10	....

2.	What is the meaning of (*f*)? _____ (*p*)? _____ (*mf*) _____	5	....
3.	What are enharmonic tones? _____	5	....
4.	Write the enharmonic tones of the following notes.	5	....

5.	What is meant by chromatic? _____	5	....
6.	This sign ¢ means _____ .	5	....
7.	A half note in (¢) time receives _____ count.	5	....
8.	What is meant by six-eight (6/8) time? _____	5	....
9.	This note in slow 6/8 time has _____ counts.	5	....
10.	The above note in fast 6/8 time has _____ counts.	5	....
11.	This note in slow 6/8 time has _____ counts. In fast time it has _____ .	5	....
12.	Mark the count under the following. Slow tempo.	5	....

| 13. | Divide the following into measures (note time signature). | 5 | .... |

14.	This sign ⁒ means _____ .	5	....
15.	In 6/8 march time (fast) the count is _____ beats to each measure.	5	....
16.	Inspection of instrument.	10	....
17.	Sight reading.	10 / 100	....

TEACHER: Write line of notes in slow six-eight time in the key of C.

B.M.Co. 11832

Scales and Arpeggios (Chords)

The material on this page may be assigned whenever the teacher feels the need for scale and chord studies. Play the following scales and chords as indicated; also play as follows:

ALWAYS NOTICE THE KEY SIGNATURE; IT IS A GUIDE FOR PROPER FINGERING:

C Major—upper octave

C Major—lower octave

G Major—one sharp: F#

D Major—two sharps: F# & C#—lower octave

D Major—upper octave

A Major—three sharps: F#, C# & G#

F Major—one flat: B♭

B♭ Major—two flats: B♭ & E♭

E♭ Major—three flats: B♭, E♭ & A♭

Chromatic Scale

B.M. Co. 11832

Onward, Christian Soldiers
(Trio)

Sir Arthur Sullivan

Vesper Hymn
(Trio)

Folk Melody

Deck the Hall
(Trio)

Welsh Air

O Little Town of Bethlehem

(Trio)

L. Redner

Silent Night

(Trio)

Franz Gruber

B.M.Co. 11832

Hark! The Herald Angels Sing

(Trio)

Felix Mendelssohn-Bartholdy